Whispers Of Valhalla

A saga of despair, redemption, and hope

J. A. Vogen

BookLeaf Publishing

India | USA | UK

Made with ❤ on the BookLeaf Publishing Platform
www.bookleafpub.in
www.bookleafpub.com

Dedication

To my amazing family, thank you for passing down your stories and sparking my creativity. And to everyone who's crossed my path, whether you stayed or taught me a lesson before moving on, thanks for giving me more stories to tell.

Preface

In my dream life, I wake before sunrise, grounded, calm, and at peace with who I've become: a woman who loves deeply without losing herself.

The fears that once held me back are nothing more than ashes now, replaced by a steady, quiet glow that lights me up from within. I am safe. I am seen. I am loved. But most importantly, I am at peace with who I've become.

I've rebuilt myself more times than I can count. These poems are fragments of midnight thoughts, raw emotions, and moments of clarity. They're the pieces that shaped the woman I am today. I've risen from the ashes, and it won't be the last time.

Acknowledgements

To the loves of my past - thank you. Each of you played a role in shaping me, whether you knew it or not. Through all the highs, the lows, and the messy in between, you helped me understand myself better and tap into emotions I didn't even know I had. Those feelings became the fuel for this book and an outlet for myself.

To my dad - thank you for keeping our Norwegian roots alive. Your stories of Viking times sparked my imagination and reminded me of where we come from.

To my mom - your endless challenges of my actions and constant push to question, reflect, and write it all down have shaped me in ways I'll always utilize.

To my brother and sister - thank you for being my sounding boards, for listening to every rant and story with open arms, and for never judging me. Your support has inspired me to be authentically myself.

To Thor, Zaylee, and Aleah - you are my brightest lights. This world is full of experiences waiting for you to explore. And if you ever feel the need to start over, know

it's always possible, and you'll have my love and support
every step of the way. I love you more than words can
ever say.

To my Jacob - my heart, my body, my soul. You see me
and understand me in ways I didn't think were possible,
in depths even I struggle to comprehend. Your love and
belief in me gave me the courage to put this book out
into the world. Words will never fully capture how much
love and respect I have for you.

Thank you all for being part of my journey and for
helping me bring life to the poems in this book.
Storytelling and poetry have always felt like they're part
of who I am, rooted in the Viking spirit.

Til Valhalla.

One.. Her

Men looked at her and thought they knew exactly what
they wanted
To be the ones to tame her passionate soul and wild
spirit.
The idea of her being the ultimate prize created a chase,
The idea of winning her over set their own ambition
ablaze.

But then, they'd get close and see behind her hazel eyes,
And what they found wasn't what they expected.
She wasn't just a pretty face or a fleeting thrill.
She was depth, passion, and a world they couldn't quite
grasp.

At first, there was belief they were up for the challenge,
That she was like any other woman,
But she wasn't. Not even close.

They tried to impress her with flashy gifts,
Lavish dinners, and trips to exquisite places.

But she didn't care about that.
She traded a thousand diamonds yearning for one real
conversation,
One moment for someone to truly know her.
One moment of true connection.

She wasn't interested in what they could buy,
Where they could take her, or the status they could
offer.
She achieved it all on her own terms.
She wanted to know them:
Who they were, what drove them, what made them tick.

That's where things started to get complicated.
Because most of them weren't ready for that.
They weren't prepared to be vulnerable, to show up
fully.
And when they realized what she wanted, they got
scared.

But that was who she was.
She wouldn't settle.
She wouldn't shrink herself to fit into someone else's
world.
She wouldn't compromise her values just to be loved,
anymore.
Starting over didn't make her skittish, she's done it

before.

To her, it was simple:
Take her as she is, or move along.
She wasn't going to change herself - not for anyone.
She knew real love would let her be exactly who she
was
And she'd wait for that, no matter how long it took.

She wasn't holding out for some fairy tale hero.
She didn't need saving or rescuing.
She slays her own dragons.
Her life was already full and beautiful,
And if love came, she'd welcome it.
If it didn't, she'd still write her own love story...her way.

So until then, she'd keep doing what she did best:
Living fully, loving fiercely, and staying true to herself.

Because no one could ever call her lonely.
She wasn't waiting; she was living.
On her own terms, in her own light.
Strong, proud, and undeniably free.

Two.. Deja Vu

In the graveyard where memories lay,
I'm haunted by echoes of yesterday,
Deja vu surrounds me, it won't let go,
The ghost of you in the afterglow.

Deja vu, playing tricks on my mind,
Walking through the cemetery of love we left behind,
Tangled emotions, like a twisted spell,
In this haunted place, where past lovers dwell.

Faded photographs, whispers in the dark,
These graveyards of memories leave a mark,
Footsteps echoing, shadows of the past,
A bittersweet reminder, love doesn't always last.

I'm standing here, staring at tombstones of trust,
The pain of old wounds, start to combust,
But I won't let this gravestone be my final place,
I'll find a way to move on, leave no trace.

We used to laugh, we used to dance,
We had a love that had a chance,
But now you're gone, it's just a memory,
And I'm left here, feeling so empty.

I'll lay these ghosts to rest, bid them farewell,
Break the chains of nostalgia, break the spell,
In this graveyard of love, I'll find my way,
To a brighter future, a brand new day.

Three.. Lost at Sea

Lost at sea, in an ocean so vast,
Searching for a shore from my distant past,
Memories of childhood, like whispers in the breeze,
But I'm drifting further away, losing pieces of me.

I'm lost at sea, can't find my way back home,
Sailing through memories, feeling so alone,
The anchor of my identity, slowly slips away,
In this vast ocean, I'm just a castaway.

I close my eyes and see glimpses of the past,
Childhood dreams, fading too fast,
The laughter, the innocence, slipping through my hands,
As I sail into the unknown, where no one understands.

The stars above guide me through the night,
But inside, I'm losing the fight,
The currents pull me farther from the shore,
Yearning for the person I was before.

But I'll keep sailing, hoping to find land,
Reclaim the pieces of myself from the sand,
For even though I'm lost, I still believe,
That one day, I'll find who I'm meant to be.

Four.. Sound the Alarm

Which way are we going? We're trapped on all sides,
Walking a minefield under bombers in the skies.
There's no escape, no path but through,
So I'll take the frontlines, all for you.

We lay in the trenches; they're closing in fast,
The air thick with danger, the plot has been cast.
I'll send the signal, we'll run for the thrill,
Against all odds, driven by will.

Because there's no one else but you,
In the chaos, my compass stays true.

Sound the alarm, the fight is near,
Through fire and storm, I'll keep you clear.
Together we stand, no matter the cost,
In this war of hearts, nothing is lost.

Five.. Tragedy

With confidence, I say, starting over paints me blue,
A silhouette hangs where clarity once stood true.
This game of tug-of-war, what do we play it for?
Both of us losing, yet neither will close the door.

Such a tragedy, staring back at me,
Two hearts betrayed, longing to break free.
I wish I had a crystal ball to show the way,
To see the chaos turn out to be beautiful one day.

The fire burns at both ends; we can't decide,
Some rise from ashes, others drown in the tide.
I never meant to keep hurting you,
But what choice was left, with nothing true?

The path less traveled seemed to fit my needs,
Yet left behind the trail of aching pleas.

It's such a tragedy, where we began so pure,
But innocence fades, leaving nothing sure.

It's such a tragedy, as we stand in the flame,
Two hearts so similar, yet neither the same.

A spark once alive now dims its glow.
As autumn fades to snow, I'm letting go.
At first a flame lit from the start,
Now I watch the embers fall apart.

Six.. Four Leaf Clover

When you search for a frame,
Only fragments remain,
Shattered pieces where the door once closed.

You lost all your beliefs,
But beneath lay four leaves,
In a patch where resilience had grown.

Disheveled and torn,
You forget why you mourn,
And wonder where I've been.

The fairy tale's gone,
But I lingered too long,
Daydreaming of what might have been.

You close both your eyes,
Drop the weight of disguise,
Trying to remember who you are.

The familiar face you see,
Is your mind's trickery,
A ghost in the scene of regret.

You search for the reason you stayed,
But the jury's dismayed,
They won't be the ones to confess.

There has to be reason,
Why do we endure this season,
When the pain is the only thing left.

Seven.. Sincere Allegations

The drive through dark to seek the light,
Against all odds, you lost the fight.
Clinging to a bittersweet surrender.

The tunnel appears, still far ahead,
As voices echo inside your head.
Trying to release all you remember.

The longest road feels shorter still,
When you have no direction, and no will.

I'll raise a glass, leave an empty chair,
Where laughter echoed, peace was there.
Recall the snowy nights on cold December.
I search the sky for signs you gave,
But no clues remain for us to save
The pieces we couldn't put together.

Sincere words twisted, allegations thrown,
A battlefield of truths unknown.

Let go of the rope, this tug-of-war,
And wonder what's worth fighting for.
Can a feeling like this last forever?

You tried it all, you gave your best,
But demons tore through walls at rest.
Hoping it would all be for the better.

Eight.. Ivory and Bone

The willow sways to the beat of a heart,
A rhythm that echoes, pulling apart.
The chants grow louder, a rising tide,
The ground shakes as shadows collide.

Nothing familiar, no solitude near,
A ghostly presence, a spirit of fear.
The chants grow louder, filling the air,
Take a look west, there's something there.

A clean strike slows my hurried pace,
I step into shadows, a fleeting embrace.
The caves are caving, yet light breaks through,
A glimpse of the western sky in view.

The whispers twist, deceit in disguise,
Promising safety, yet breeding lies.
Let go of the weight that drags you low,
If you ever want wings, let it all go.

Erase your thoughts, take a deep breath,
Feel the rhythm that beats in your chest.
The chants grow louder, filling your mind,
Calling you forward, leaving fear behind.

Ease your soul, trust the path ahead,
Feel the rhythm, let go of dread.
The chants grow louder, steady and clear,
A song of courage that draws you near.

The chants are rising, the rhythm divine,
A call to soar, to claim what's mine.

Nine.. Golden Hour

The thrill of connection, a spark inside,
A deeper dive where secrets hide.
Fear of rejection, butterflies' disguise,
Let it burn, let it all rise.

Damage control, a pawn in the game,
Close the book or tear every page.
No stories left, no roles to play,
Let it burn, take it all away.

There's a price to freedom, a heavy toll,
Perspective's the gold that binds the soul.
A purgatory built with my own hands,
Fear of the unknown still commands.
Let it burn, let the world ignite,
A fire consuming the endless night.

Up in flames, the golden hour,
Reflections dance, a fleeting power.
Five hundred fifty stories high,

A match struck beneath the sky.
Watch the blaze climb higher still,
An untamed force, bending will.

Let it burn, let it all burn,
Ashes to ashes, no need to return.
Higher and higher, the fire's embrace,
A cleansing flame to leave no trace.

Ten.. Satellites

Satellites spin, orbiting high,
Lost in the vast expanse of the sky.
Into the unknown, the endless abyss.
If we never find it, there's nothing to miss.

Trapped in routine, the same every day,
Between the stars, where light fades away.
A fire burns, like the sun's fierce glow,
But venture too close, and the wings let go.

The aftermath of disaster gleams,
A misleading light, the glow of dreams.

Fight or flight, it's all the same,
Stay too long, or leave the flame.
A crystal ball, your fate unfolds,
Wait for a sign, a truth untold.

Wishful thoughts lead nowhere fast,
Only action can outlast.

Trust feels brittle, followed by scars,
From battles fought beneath the stars.

Bridges burn as tables turn,
Each pain is just a lesson learned.
If you could take it back, extinguish the spark,
Would you leave with no trace, no mark?

Thinking there's purpose, searching for signs,
A hope that lingers in the lines.

Eleven.. Thieves

I tried to stay away, unseen through my lover's eyes,
But caught your guard down, a spark I couldn't disguise.
I knew you'd glance my way, your gaze a steady flame,
And in that moment, I knew I'd set your world aflame.
You're the rarest gold I've ever tried to claim.

Each night, I see you when I close my eyes,
This shallow heart of mine still holds surprise.
Like fine wine sipped slow, you leave me in a daze,
Hold me close; I'll never stray.

Like a thief vanishes into the darkest night,
We didn't know our match would burn so bright.
If I had known the fire would last this long,
I might've thought twice before asking for your light.
Now in the afterglow, our memories take flight.

We knew the risk, the danger we held,
But the pull between us was something we'd never felt.
Straight into the storm, no chance in sight.

We brought a gun to a knife fight.

I push you away, yet you pull me near,
This shallow heart of mine still holds you, dear.
Like fine wine sipped slow, you leave me in a haze,
Hold me close; I'll never stray.

I was a thief, and I slipped through your door,
Stole your breath, left you begging for more.
Caught your guard down in that fleeting light,
Now we both burn in the fire we ignite.

Twelve.. The Piano Man

The room was quiet, the world stood still,
Saved for the notes that bent to his will.
Softly they flowed from the piano's frame,
Each one a whisper, each one a flame.

It lingers in pauses, in moments that stay,
In the way his eyes spark just before he plays.
His hands wove a melody, air turned to sound,
Each note a truth my heart had just found.

I crossed to the window, arms folded tight,
Shielding myself from the pull of his light.
What does your soul sing of? I dared to say,
His answer came swift, with no thought to delay.

Of you, he replied, his gaze so clear,
The melody I seek, the song I hold, dear.
The world outside blurred, time ceased to exist,
Drawn by the gravity of his insist.

Then his lips met mine, warm and sure,
A harmony timeless, tender, and pure.
Not just a kiss, but a life set alight,
A melody now burning inside me to be his wife.

Thirteen.. Forest Fires

In the heat of the moment, our worlds collide,
A spark ignited, scrutiny amplified.
A fleeting connection, we danced through the night,
But the flames grew higher, no end in sight.

Caught up in the chaos, we lost control,
Passion burning like a forest in full glow.
Whispered secrets in the flickering light,
Can we see past the trees around us, just for one night.

We set the night on fire.
Two souls intertwined.
Amidst the ashes, we found our desire,
But the flames grew higher, the flames grew higher.

We were wild and reckless, lost in the haze,
Unleashing into a fiery blaze.
The forest whispered secrets, as we explored,
Underneath the moonlit sky, we soared.

Now the embers fade, but the memories remain,
A night of passion that won't be in vain.
No judgment, no shame, we lived in the now,
And as the flames die down, we take our bow.

In the aftermath, as we go our separate ways,
The forest fire still burns in our hearts ablaze.
No regrets, no looking back, we'll always remember,
The time we embraced the warmth of December.

Fourteen.. Midnight Train

Running away on a midnight train,
To the city that never sleeps, where dreams remain.
With every step I take, a story unfolds,
In this concrete jungle, I break the mold.

In the shadows of doubt, I found my escape,
A restless spirit, a phoenix rising from ash.
The wheels roll on, as the city unfolds,
I'm ready to escape, to vanish.

The skyline beckons, like a distant memory.
I step into the streets, a stranger amidst the sea.
A kaleidoscope of faces, blending in the crowd.
I still see you somehow.

The pulse of my heartbeat, the rhythm of the tracks.
Footsteps echoing, shadows of the past,
The memories of who I was, like the setting sun,
Ready, set, it's time to run.

In the depths of the city, my spirit took flight,
A symphony of dreams, sparkling through the night.
I shed my old skin, memories of who I used to be,
Walking through these streets, I'll finally be free.

Fifteen.. Concrete Jungle

Feel the heat when you're too near the fire,
Dancing with demons who know your desires.
Sell your soul for a mantra, a fleeting guide,
But it's the surest way to lose all inside.

Life moves fast, a relentless spin,
With cigarettes burning down in Brooklyn.
Fade away in the concrete maze,
Awake till dawn in a transient haze.

Freedom feels real, but the moment is brief,
Open your eyes, and it turns to grief.
A cigarette burns both within and without,
A restless soul with ancestral doubt.

Brick by brick, an empire is made,
But in a blink, it can crumble and fade.
A spirit awakened, a fire untamed,
A reminder of all we must release, unchained.

Chasing passions without knowing their end,
Feeding obsessions, content left to bend.
Adrenaline rushes, it courses, it reigns,
Yet how do we progress, unearthing the pain?

Fade away in the concrete sprawl,
Where shadows stretch, and towers fall.
To move forward, we must recall -
Where we've come from, or lose it all.

Sixteen.. Penthouse

Standing atop the world so high,
Ten thousand stories touch the sky.
Everyone below looks small,
And every problem fades, that's all.
This is who you're meant to be,
Life tugging gently, setting you free.

A placeholder in the in between,
Of where you've been and what you've seen.

Time slips by in the blink of an eye,
Seasons shift, old habits die.
You can lead a horse to the stream,
But you can't make it chase it's dream.
You can do your best, give all you've got,
But being the hero isn't always your spot.
One thing stands, forever true -
Happiness looks so good on you.

Floating softly, a cloud beneath,

Flying free, no chains to sheath.
The world below moves at light's pace,
A blur of moments, a fleeting race.
What's happened to you, near and far,
Has brought you here, just as you are.

Seventeen.. Goodbye

Time is driving me out of my mind,
Every face I meet brings you to mind.
Your eyes, your smile, the way you'd stay,
How does fire just fade away?

From hearts ablaze to a quiet fall,
Time and space, I've questioned it all.
Distance whispers what I now know true,
It only makes me long for you.

I understand why you had to leave,
This life of mine was hard to conceive.
I'm tied for now, but February's near,
Waiting for love feels unclear.

Still, those months we shared woke me inside,
Brought me back to life, renewed my stride.
The chase, the thrill, the way you'd glow,
You lit a spark I didn't know.

But coping was messy, and I lost my way,
Drunk texts and silence, we pushed each other away.
I couldn't move on, no matter how I tried,
But I'd have sunk us both if I'd stayed by your side.

For now, I release you, I set you free,
Letting go of what can't yet be.
But deep in my heart, you'll always stay,
A piece of me that won't fade away.

Eighteen. . Choices

I lit a cigarette, smoke curled in the night,
You smiled, half smirk, in the neon light.

Our baggage could sink us; no one would care.
It'd be easier to leave it all there.

But silence fell heavy, and yet, we stayed,
Two hearts unsure, but unwilling to fade.

Maybe we've met our match this time,
Maybe we're facing what's left behind.

It's terrifying, you know, to hang by a thread,
Knowing one word could leave both of us dead.

But still, there's something I can't ignore,
Something deeper, something more.

Even with chaos, I want you near.
The mess, the scars, they brought me here.

The silence was full, no words left to say,
Yet your eyes told me all in their quiet way.

I used to think love should be easy and clear,
But it's about choosing, even through fear.

In you, I saw every version, every truth,
Baggage and all, I choose us, I choose you.

Nineteen.. Take the High Road

Two paths diverge, a choice to weigh,
Will you walk the high road today?
Two hearts stir, but it's far too late,
Will you rise above, or tempt your fate?

Self control, a familiar shield,
Yet this righteous road no joy can yield.
I've grown so weary, so cold, so bored -
Why keep a promise I can't afford?
No more will I tread the virtuous track,
The high road's lost; there's no turning back.

Full speed ahead to nowhere fast,
If nothing gold stays, we'll make it last.
The chase ignites, I'm coming undone,
Deception's a thrill when you're on the run.
A heart that beats will surely ache,
When tension mounts and raises stakes.

One kiss exchanged, mistakes collide,
We abandon the high road, side by side.
Spiraling out of control, we stray,
No thoughts of righteousness block our way.
Never again will the high road call,
For we've chosen to risk it all.

Open doors we can't unseal,
Hearts about to crack, to feel.
We dance around a danger untamed,
A trigger pulled leaves none unclaimed.
Stories spread, the stones will fly,
Your spark ignites, the flames climb high.
The deck is laid, the cards are shown,
This fire consumes what's left unknown.

A heart that beats is bound to break,
But still, we race with love at stake.
The bullets fly, the moments won't last,
If nothing gold stays, let's burn it fast.

Twenty.. The End

We knew each other once before,
A shattered window, a party's roar.
I danced on tables, wild and free,
Then life froze still: for you, for me.
Star crossed lovers, paths anew,
Your other, my other, betrayal brewed.
But life moves forward, hearts repair,
They found their joy; we found ours there.
Eight years passed, a handshake froze,
The second time that life would close.
Your eyes, so brown, so fiercely kind,
Unlocked the memories in my mind.
Cigarettes and whiskey haze,
A spark ignited through the maze.
Your laugh, a sound I'd keep for years,
A remedy to keep for future tears.
Flash forward now, time stops once more,
A kiss that breaks and can't restore.
Life happens, then you live, it's true,
And neither one of us could follow through.

Twenty-One.. Phoenix

She'd rebuilt herself from the ashes more than once,
Each time stronger, each time brighter.
And like a phoenix, she soared, untouchable and free.

Men tried to capture her brilliance,
But they only burned in the glow of her flames.
Some thought they could cage her fire,
Others thought they could dim her light.
But none understood her essence.
She was born to rise, not to be contained.

One man, brave enough to crave,
Reached out to hold the fire in his hands.
But he learned the truth the hard way:
A phoenix doesn't stay for those who fear the heat.
She only lingers for those who dare to burn beside her.

And so she flew on, her wings glistening with untapped
power,
Searching not for a captor, but an equal,

Someone who wouldn't try to extinguish her fire,
But would instead bring their own to meet hers.

Until then, she would keep rising,
Higher and brighter with every fall.
For she was a phoenix, and no man, no matter how bold,
Had ever been able to catch her.
She was never yours to hold.